Jungle Olympics

800 Metres Sprint

Aqkay

Published By Galaxy Books
Copyright © 2016 Aqkay
All rights reserved.

ISBN: 0-9935428-1-6
ISBN-13: 978-0-9935428-1-7

"Why are you running so fast?" asked Mr Goat; "I know you are a deer and you like to run very fast, but please let me keep pace with you."

"All right, I will try," said Mr Deer but instead of slowing down, he ran even faster while leaping in the air.

"Oh no, "cried Mr Goat, "Now you are flying too!"

"You know, the wind is behind me, "said Mr Deer; "I cannot help leaping high up, it is such fun!"

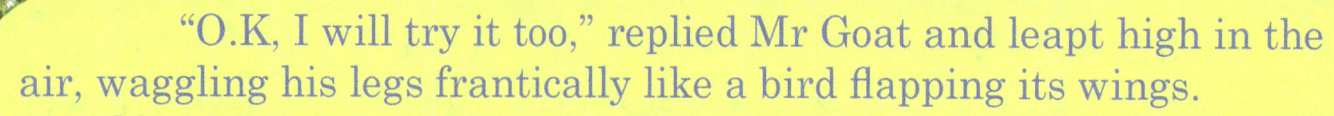

"O.K, I will try it too," replied Mr Goat and leapt high in the air, waggling his legs frantically like a bird flapping its wings.

"Oh, Mama," cried Mr Goat. Instead of flying, he'd had a nasty fall. It was a bad stroke of luck for Mr Goat that Mr Cat, Mr Rabbit and Mr Dog had been watching him. They were wondering what was wrong with Mr Goat.

"Trying a long jump, Mr Goat?" said Mr Cat playfully, "That was almost a world record."

"London Olympics are only a few years ahead," laughed Mr Rabbit, "If you can jump like this, you must take part and represent us."

"Next time you try to fly so high," barked Mr Dog, "remember to open your parachute before you descend."

Mr Goat felt very bad. Although not seriously hurt, he was bruised a little, but those nasty remarks pained him a lot more. Normally he enjoyed the respect of his fellow animals, who usually considered him very wise. He had to do or say something to justify his stupid jump. Mr Rabbit's mention of London Olympics gave him an idea.

"Sorry mates, I was practicing for the Jungle Olympics," shouted Mr Goat, "I intend to take part in the high jump event you know."

"JUNGLE OLYMPICS?" they all shouted back.
"Yes. We are going to hold the Jungle Olympics here very soon. Better get ready for them." replied Mr Goat.

It was a midsummer afternoon in the far off forest, hundreds of miles away from any big city. There was green grass everywhere and the trees were laden with fruits. There was plenty of food for every bird and animal. It was their daily routine to wake up, eat and drink, go back to sleep again or stretch out in the cool shade of a nice spreading tree.

But there was one big drawback - they were starting to get very lazy and life was becoming monotonous. Something had to be done to bring back the excitement to their lives. Mr Goat's idea of holding an Olympic event was a winner. Everybody accepted it most enthusiastically. There was no need for discussion.

In the meantime a lot of other animals and birds had become curious and closed in to join the crowd.

"When will the Olympics start?" asked Mr Lion, "I hope I will be the president of the Olympic committee."

"Who is in the organisation committee?" enquired Mr Fox, "Please do not forget me."

"What about the security?" shouted Mr Bear," Let me take care of it."

"I am sure you will choose me as the Olympic judge," said Mr Owl, "I know all the rules and my eyesight is excellent."

Each bird and animal wished to get involved and enjoy it. Excitement was so high that everyone wanted the Jungle Olympics to start as soon as possible. After a while they agreed that, since the day was still young and there was plenty of time till sunset, they could hold at least one event right away. They decided to start the Jungle Olympics immediately.

"Which event should we start now?" asked Mr Lion, "It should be a good one!"

"800 metres sprint!" shouted Mr Rabbit before anyone could reply, "I will take part in this event."

"That is an interesting event!" said Mr Lion, "Let us start with it. Who will race with Mr Rabbit?"

Everyone knew that Mr Rabbit was the fastest runner in the forest. Mr Parrot, who watched him running from up above the tree, thought that he ran as fast as lightning and may be faster. There was a lull in the crowd; nobody wanted to be humiliated in defeat.

"Count me in!" said a thin voice.

They all looked around; nobody could see who was talking.

"I will race with Mr Rabbit!" shouted the thin voice again, "Look down under Mr Wolf. I am here."

Everyone looked down, frowning. They saw Mr Turtle crouched under Mr Wolf.

The crowd burst into a loud peal of laughter!

Were they laughing to see Mr Turtle, the slowest animal amongst them, wanting to compete in a 800 metres sprint against the fastest animal in the forest?

No, they were absolutely not. They were laughing because it was a favourite joke of theirs. The joke, which had become known world-wide. Who does not know the story about a race between a hare and a tortoise and its result?

Well, Mr Rabbit was the hare and Mr Turtle, the tortoise of that story.

"O.K, you are on. Any more entries?" roared Mr Lion, the self-appointed president of the Olympic committee.

A hush descended over the crowd. None replied.

"Let us find more contestants," shouted Mr Goat, "The race will not be so thrilling with only two participants."

They screwed up their eyes and frowned around.

"Mr Horse and Mr Deer are not here," said Mr Fox, "They are both good sprinters. I am sure they will like to take part in this event. Let us search for them and ask them to enter this contest."

"All right," roared the self-appointed president of the Olympic committee,

"Entry to this event is still open. Anyone who wishes to take part should submit his name to the Olympic committee within one hour." Mr Goat, Mr Fox and Mr Owl exited hastily to search for Mr Horse and Mr Deer.

Mr Rabbit felt quite relieved. He remembered how he had lost the race and the frustration, anger and humiliation he suffered afterwards. He had tried several times to have a re-race but Mr Turtle avoided it somehow.
 "Now," he said to himself, "I will win the race by a big margin and wash away that stain of humiliation!"

Mr Horse was a thoroughbred. His pedigree could be traced to more than three generations. With his long slender body, well-chiselled head on a long neck, high withers, deep chest, short back, depth of hindquarters, and long legs, he was a true picture of a race horse.

He used to take part in big horse races. Like all thoroughbred racehorses he performed with maximum effort, which can be very dangerous. Eventually he, himself, had been injured in a racing accident and declared unfit for any further races. Confined to a stable, he finally got so miserable he ran away to the forest where he'd been welcomed by all the other animals and had become well integrated. Everyone liked him. He, too, was very friendly with all of them.

But Mr Horse had a secret. Maybe due to the fuss during the previous racing contests, which he really didn't enjoy, or to the accident or whatever, he absolutely *loathed* running!

Now Mr Deer, on the other hand, simply loved sprinting. He particularly enjoyed sprinting when the wind was behind him. It was always a joy to watch him running and then kick-bouncing into the air as if he was flying. But Mr Deer had one tiny fault, too. Although he was a very lovable and kind creature, he could also be extremely stubborn. Once he had made up his mind to do something, he would stick to that decision no matter what.

Mr Horse and Mr Deer were very good friends. In fact, they enjoyed each oth er's company so much that they spent most of their time together. Mr Horse liked Mr Deer's simple naivety. Mr Deer respected Mr Horse because of his travels and experience in the tough world of racing arenas. As Mr Deer had never travelled outside the forest, he never got tired of listening to Mr Horse's exciting stories about distant places called cities and racing adventures.

This was what Mr Deer was doing. He was listening to Mr Horse's latest tale of a thrilling horse race which was about to finish.

"Oh, here you both are," said Mr Goat, "Thank goodness we found you. We were searching for you everywhere."

Totally absorbed in the story, neither Mr Horse nor Mr Deer took any notice of him at first.

"Hurry up, both of you, you have to enrol yourselves for the Olympic sprint event." shouted Mr Owl urgently.

"What is an Olympic?" asked Mr Deer.

"Olympic sprint event!" muttered Mr Horse, "In this thick forest?"

"Yes, we are holding an Olympic sprint event here and there is very little time left before entry is closed." said Mr Fox, "hurry up! Let us go and register your names."

"Over my dead body," cried Mr Horse, "You know I hate running. Sorry, mate. Count me out."

Mr Fox had anticipated this answer. But Mr Fox was very foxy indeed, and he had a plan.

He knew that Mr Horse was desperate to acquire the nationality of a genuine forest dweller. He had applied for it to the Jungle Council but, as he had not been resident in the forest for five years, he'd so-far been refused.

"You know, Mr Horse; this is not simply a question of prestige. If you win the race you will get a gold medal and, as an Olympic gold medal holder, you will automatically qualify for the nationality."

"Is that so?" asked Mr Horse of the others, looking doubtful.

"YES" shouted Mr Owl, Mr Fox and Mr Goat together," We guarantee it."

"O.K," said Mr Horse uneasily, "Then I will take part in this event."

"And what about you, Mr Deer?" asked Mr Goat," Will you also take part?"

"If my friend Mr Horse is taking part," replied Mr Deer, "I will too. Just for the fun of it."

"Thank you very much," said Mr Fox, secretly smiling to himself. "Let us hurry and get your names enrolled."

They dashed towards the registration office, reached it just in time, and duly registered Mr Horse and Mr Deer as contestants in the Olympic sprint event.

"O.K, time is up now, no more entries," roared Mr Lion," let the race begin!"

The preparations for the 800 metres sprint event began. It was decided that the contestants would run up to a 400 metres mark and then back to the starting point again. Starting and finishing points were marked with a line and then Mr Crow was asked to fly 400 metres in a straight line and then mark the metres distance. A line was drawn at metres that end.

Crowds gathered both at the start and 400 metres marks.
Mr Rabbit ran to stand confidently at the start line, Mr Horse galloped and Mr Deer jumped to join him. Mr Turtle, on the other hand, crept very slowly while everyone else waited impatiently.
Firstly there was a pin-drop silence then the crowd started to chant, "Ready, steady, set and …."
"GO!" roared Mr Lion.
The Jungle Olympics 800 metres sprint event had begun.

Mr Rabbit darted like a flash of light. He ran so fast that Mr Parrot, who was watching him from a tree at the start line, thought that he was even faster than the lightning.

Mr Horse and Mr Deer sprinted extremely fast, too. At first they were neck to neck with Mr Rabbit. It was a hot gusty day and the contestants had to run against the wind. Mr Deer was not enjoying the sprint at all. When he leapt high, he fell like a stone; there was no wind from behind to carry him forward. Even worse: the stiff breeze coming from ahead was damping his flight during the jump. He toiled for a while but it was no fun.

Mr Horse was sprinting because sprinting was what he was trained to do. Joy or no joy, that was his function and he was automatically doing it. All the same, Mr Rabbit was giving him quite a contest. In fact Mr Rabbit was about to overtake him and win the race.

"Hey, listen!" heard Mr Horse.

He looked to his side, Mr Deer was directing him to get away from the track and enter a grove of trees.

Mr Deer ran into the grove of trees. Mr Horse followed uncertainly.

"What on earth are we doing?" shouted Mr Horse, "What about the race. I was about to win it."

"Oh, do you think so!" replied Mr Deer," Were you enjoying it? I really hated it."

"Me too," laughed Mr Horse," You are right. It was a real torture. Nationality or no nationality, we quit."

"What about the other animals," said Mr Horse, "What will we say to Mr Goat to explain why we abandoned the race?"

"We will tell them that we had lost our way," replied Mr Deer with a wry smile, "It was their duty to mark the track well. You see there are no signs here."

"Yes, of course." replied Mr Horse, "It is so easy to lose your way here, I suppose. Otherwise I would have won the event, you realize?"

"Absolutely, you would have done," said Mr Deer with a wink," After all; you are a thoroughbred race horse, are you not?"

They burst into loud laughter….

Mr Rabbit reached the 400 metres mark within minutes. The crowd cheered him. He looked back. There was no sign of Mr Turtle. He had seen Mr Horse and Mr Deer abandoning the race. Now, it appeared, it was only a race between him and Mr Turtle.

He looked even harder, but Mr Turtle was definitely not there. He began to run back to the start line but then stopped after about 150 metres.

"Why hurry?" he thought. "It's already obvious that I am the fastest sprinter. If I run back as fast as I can, the race will be over in a few minutes. I will be a winner, but then as a good sportsman, I will never be able to taunt Mr Turtle in front of the others. I will never be able to humiliate that slow-coach adversary in a way I have been humiliated for so long after losing our last race."

Mr Rabbit had started to have a notion that the race had become one sided and boring. He decided to wait for Mr Turtle's arrival, tease him to his heart's content, then run back in triumph.

The sun was blazing hot now. Mr Rabbit felt far too warm after running so fast in that heat. He looked around. There were a lot of farms nearby. The nearest farm looked very cool and inviting. He strolled into it and checked what was growing there. His eyes began to glitter and his mouth started to water.

It was a carrot farm. Thousands of fat, juicy carrots were all around him.

Mr Rabbit had two passions. One of them was carrots. Whenever he saw carrots, he threw all caution to the wind and went after them. To Mr Rabbit, carrots were positively irresistible.

He started to eat carrot after carrot. One, two, three, four, five, six…… Then he stopped counting and simply ate and ate till his stomach sagged down to the ground like a big sack of potatoes. No matter how desperately he wanted to eat more he could not. He really had to stop.

By then, let alone running and running fast, he found difficulty in even moving. His tummy started to ache whenever he tried to walk, never mind run.

"Twenty carrots were yummy … but now I have an ache in my tummy" sang Mr Rabbit, laughing heartily nevertheless.

He looked for Mr Turtle again, but Mr Turtle was still not there.

"I have plenty of time, "he thought. 'So why don't I rest for a while and become fit again?"

There was a nice shaded nook under an apple tree. It was very inviting. Mr Rabbit decided to rest under it for a little while. Just a very little while.

I told you that Mr Rabbit had two passions. One, you already know, was carrots, his other passion was sleep. He loved sleeping for hours and hours even for days… especially when his tummy was full, like it was now.

He crept into that inviting, shady den. He'd fallen asleep before he hit the ground.

Standing at the start line, Mr Turtle looked at his formidable opponents. There was a racehorse, a deer who not only runs very fast, but flies as well, and his old rival, the well-known sprinter, Mr Rabbit. His heart started to sink.

"My goodness," thought Mr Turtle, "What am I doing here?"

Then he remembered why he had entered his name for the competition. This was the first ever Jungle Olympics. If he took part in them, he would be remembered by his children and the next generations as the "Turtle who ran in the Olympics".

When the race started, his opponents whizzed past him like bullets and vanished beyond the horizon, leaving only puffs of dust which made his eyes water.

Mr Turtle started to creep forward, as fast as his legs could carry him. He was very aware that 800 metres was a long distance to go for a turtle. His legs were not designed for running fast: they were much better for swimming, but he carried on.

The ever-widening gap between him and the other contestants was so immense that the crowd started to taunt him.

"Come on, get moving," shouted someone in the crowd," You do not have to take so long in starting, you are not a diesel motor."

"Don't mind us, "shouted another, "We'll wait. Hopefully you will be back in our life time."

Mr Turtle carried on creeping forward centimetre by centimetre. His legs had started to hurt, and the weight of the shell on his back had become unbearable. He was getting so tired and the distance was appearing so long, that he started to think about quitting the race.

"Winning is fantastic," he remembered his mother saying," but participation is a great honour too. Whenever you take part in a contest, give your best and leave the rest to God. Don't ever give up."

He drew strength from that happy memory. Mr Turtle, despite his aches and pains, started moving steadily and relatively faster.

After a long, long time and great toil he'd reached the 400 metre mark. There were only a few spectators there now. Most of them had left. When they saw Mr Turtle they started to mock him.

"Go home," shouted Mr Jackal," Mr Rabbit was here hours ago. He must have won the race by now."

"I did not see him sprinting back," replied Mr Turtle uncertainly.

"He was running so fast," shouted someone, "he must have become invisible".They laughed heartily.

"Come what may," replied Mr Turtle stubbornly," I have a job to do and I will finish it anyhow."

"Bravo!" shouted the line umpire," Go on and finish the race."

Mr Turtle gathered all his strength and started his wearisome journey back to the finishing line. He was very tired but strangely he did not feel so bad now. He had started to enjoy this epic adventure. After all he was taking part in an Olympic event, which was a great feat for anyone, let alone a small forest turtle. He decided to concentrate on the sprint, forget about the crowd, winning or losing.

When he reached near his goal, he began to hear loud shouts from the crowd. He decided not to pay any attention, just to keep on creeping forward.

At last, he crossed the finishing line. The lion started roaring. He heard such loud shouting from the crowd that his ears became deaf to them. He could not understand a single word that they were saying. Mr Turtle thought that he was being ridiculed for being so slow. Better not to hear their taunts and insults. But then he realized that something was different. The crowd was CHEERING, not jeering.

They gathered around him, congratulated him and tried to pick him up and hug him. Mr Turtle was so confused that he did not grasp the significance of all the fuss. He withdrew his head into his shell like turtles do when they are anxious.

"SILENCE!" roared Mr Lion," Silence please. If anybody shouts now, I will eat him!"

All of a sudden, the crowd became absolutely still. It was so quiet that one could hear the wind sighing in the trees.

"Now, Olympic Secretary Mr Owl will declare the results of the Jungle Olympics 800 metres sprint event," roared Mr Lion." Please keep quiet and listen carefully!"

"Hoop!" Mr Owl cleared his throat," The winner of Jungle Olympics 800 metres sprint event is … Mr TURTLE!"

The crowd started to cheer, shout, dance and congratulate Mr Turtle.

Mr Turtle realized, almost with horror at first, that the unbelievable had happened. He had WON!

Until, gradually, he became so happy that his happiness knew no bounds, whereupon a strange calmness descended over him. He realized that it was the one moment he would cherish all his life and he should enjoy it….which was precisely what he began to do.

He was asked to come forward, stand on the victory stand and receive the gold medal for the Jungle Olympics 800 metres sprint event.

While he was receiving the gold medal the forest's national anthem was played. He thought about his moments of despair during the race and realized that it was his steadfastness, his commitment and his perseverance which had brought him to this stand. He could easily have given up, but whoever dares, wins.

After the prize-giving ceremony, a big party started. All the animals, including those who were taunting him, tried to get his autograph and have their pictures taken with him.

It was a moment of great joy for Mr Turtle. He was a worthy winner of an Olympic gold medal. His name would be written in the Jungle Olympic record book. His sprint time (2 hours 55 minutes 42 seconds) was the Olympics 800 metre sprint record time. It would stand till broken in the next Olympics.

Mr Turtle remembered his family and wanted to go back to them and inform them about his achievement. He started to creep towards his home. The crowd followed him, but progress was very slow. Very slow indeed. The crowd were finding real difficulty going at Mr Turtle's pace.

"Can I pick you up, please?" shouted Mr Elephant," Everyone wants to see you anyway, and we'll all move a bit quicker"

Secretly grateful, Mr Turtle agreed. Mr Elephant picked him up and placed him on his head.

The procession started moving again towards Mr Turtle's home. Everyone was singing, dancing and cheering. It was such fun that Mr Lion declared they would hold the Jungle Olympics as an annual festival, not just every four years like the Humans did.

Mr Rabbit slept well and long. Suddenly the unmistakable bellow of a lion in the distance startled him into wakefulness. It took him a moment to realize that all the animals were cheering and Mr Lion was roaring like mad. He opened his eyes. It was late evening by then, and the sun had begun to set. His mind slowly cleared as he remembered that he'd been running a race with his old rival, Mr Turtle.

He realized that all the commotion was to cheer Mr Turtle when he crossed the finishing line to become first home.

"I have done it AGAIN, blow it!" thought Mr Rabbit, "For the second time I have been defeated by a slow but steady turtle."

He saw no point in getting up. He still had his den and the "carrot paradise". Mr Rabbit simply shrugged, and went to sleep again.

Did he dream of having yet another re-race with Mr Turtle?

You tell me …?

ABOUT THE AUTHOR

Aqkay lives in Wallington, Greater London, U.K. He enjoys writing poetry, Children's stories and short stories. He has written 3 poetry books. "Echoes" a collection of poems, "Jharna" Urdu/Hindi poetry books and "Sing and Play" a collection of poems with pictures for children aged 5-10 . He has also written a science fiction "The Boss" and 3 story books, "Jungle Olympics-800 Metres Sprint" , "Jungle Olympics-Wrestling Free Style" and "Jungle Olympics-Cricket" of the Jungle Olympics series for children aged 5-10.

www.ingramcontent.com/pod-product-compliance
Lightning Source LLC
Chambersburg PA
CBHW080519020526
44113CB00055B/2533